Advance

as if to return m

CH00927020

"Is there a consciousness beyond ale[...]
wildfire is the sun's incessant spotligh[...] [...] [...]ings living and struggling. Richards' poems are an immersive travelog with a blood imagination, a love letter beneath open sky, exposed to the elements, where all poetry is self-help, is the collapse and ballooning of a self like a lung. Her poetic pulse reveals emotional biomes, without turning away from the spirit's gash, testing her idea that nature is not the cure, just the medicine." — Dot Devota, Author of *And The Girls Worried Terribly*

"Kristen Noelle Richards' as if to return myself to the sea is a love letter to wanderlust. It is a collection of poems that collides the mundane experiences—capturing them in an essence of divinity—and the existential ruminations that sometimes plague us as human beings. Kristen Noelle Richards' debut poetry collection is a heartfelt, warm hug to the wanderer, globetrotter, and gypsy in all of us." — Flor Ana, Author of *A Moth Fell In Love With The Moon*

"This book is for every wild woman who is still trying to find purpose and self-love, and growing roots between the modern world and the natural one. Kristen Noelle Richards's poetry reminds you that you're not alone and that the only way to discover your place is to keep trekking, exploring, and reflecting until it starts to make sense." — Annie Vazquez, Author of *My Little Prayer Book: 75 Prayers, Poems and Mantras for Illumination*

"*as if to return myself to the sea* beholds a beautiful intuition that is observant, delicate, and striking in its connection between the natural and human condition. It possesses a thirst for wonder and bewilderment unlike anything I have experienced. Diving into the in-between of survival, life, and desire, Richards explores her existence in a surreal, playful, and articulate manner." — Finn Mott, Author of *Call Me Disturbing: A Story About COVID 19, Cancer, Relationships, America, and Hope*

"This is one of the most beautiful, well written poetry collections I have read in a long time. Kristen Noelle Richards navigates a very real and relatable sense of longing through a sea of emotions and the vivid imagery of her travels. Her words are strong, meaningful, and will strike your heart strings from the first poem. Richards has compiled an amazing collection here that I highly recommend!" — dsb.poetry, Author of *We Were Fire in the Night*

"Drawing inspiration from her immersive hiking experiences around Lake Tahoe, Richards eloquently explores the profound interconnectedness between the body, the mind, and the natural world. With evocative imagery and introspective musings, Richards takes readers on a transformative journey as she contemplates the fragility of existence and the longing for new experiences and identities. as if to return myself to the sea is a lyrical exploration that will leave readers breathless, yearning for more of Richards' captivating verses that invite readers to reflect on the fleeting moments and the profound wonder that surrounds us all." — Oscar Fuentes, Author of *Honey & Sting*

"Kristen Noelle Richards brings an immersive experience to my body as I read through her poems in *as if to return myself to the sea*. I melt into the earth around me as if I too, am returning myself to the sea. Her words stretch my limbs over mountains and oceans and make me feel even more, that I am purely a part of nature." — Kendall Hope, Author of *The Willow Weepings*

"Kristen Noelle Richards questions the connections between the internal and external world, the pathways between nature and nurture, and the space between the corporeal and our spirit. Using grammar to simulate the blurring of boundaries, the imagery in these poems transition from the specific settings of her everyday world, such as pick-up trucks and fields just outside of Portland, to the existential abstracts of burning minds beside the absence of water, while the author searches for herself and her purpose in this threshold space." — Renzo Del Castillo, Author of *Still*

"*as if to return myself to the sea* is an intricately painted landscape that dives into scenic trains of thought by the author. Richards writes to her younger self and encapsulates the feeling of growing beyond the past. This collection is truly a must read!" — Tiffany Rose Allen, Author of *At The Beginning Of Yesterday*

as if to return myself
to the sea

kristen noelle richards

Cover Art Copyright © 2023 by Alli Broderick

Edited by Flor Ana Mireles

1st Edition | 01
Paperback ISBN: 979-8-9880379-1-0

First Published August 2023

For inquiries and bulk orders, please email:
indieearthpublishinghouse@gmail.com

Printed in the United States

1 2 3 4 5 6 7 8 9

Indie Earth Publishing Inc.
| Miami, FL |

INDIE EARTH
PUBLISHING

as if to return myself to the sea

Kristen Richards

contents

for my grandfather

only to the degree that we expose ourselves
over and over to annihilation
can that which is destructible in us
be found.

- Pema Chörön

the growing place

where i can think myself water

i am daring to make life one long eclipse of lightning bugs
in a field outside portland where summer heat
laughs our sweat dry; we are waiting
for the apples to grow red, for time to move
and it does, it moves so fast and so sweet
it moves across all of maine just to meet me
at the sea, for one last goodbye, before
i return myself, eyes and childhood wide with wonder
i am grasping for sandcastles i built here
for what i buried in this dirt. departing
without roots is the scariest thing i have ever done
here i am going west, not to the sea, an ocean
made of salt, where just with memories
i can think myself water in the middle of the desert

the only body left dancing

here is the growling of a pick-up truck, its noise eats
bird songs, makes me look for the time and wonder
with the knowing *i am neglecting something to be here*
but today there is no one coming to meet me on the side
of a state highway along the california
and nevada border. no, i see places as the most intimate
clothing we will *ever* wear, but where i define home
is a shaky birch a few miles too close to a wildfire always
moving south, anticipation to be somewhere fast, as if
i could write about this running forever, it is all
i have let myself know. i don't have to believe
my reflection if i'm always changing time zones
if i'm always putting on sunscreen with gravel in my palms
if i settle too much, and the sun gets to know me
i will start measuring my thighs in her shadow, judging
my femininity by its ability to be left unacknowledged
the farther i go from the engine exhaust, where
the burning smoke is my dusty steps, i realize
the only thing i will every truly own is my body
and how i keep turning it
displacing it with someone else's skin, i can
write myself a hundred love songs and not believe
any of them, except the last when i am
the only one left dancing.

as if to return myself to the sea

when i get there, the first place i go is home
to my body, how it sobs in heat, forgets
how to sing anything but the hum of its own heartbeat
i sit in the dirt to wonder at these bones, to ask them
how it feels to lay rock on rock and let it all scatter
as the granite crumbles. sand, i say, is what
my body will become once i finally run it out, as if to
return myself to the sea, answer only in dampened cursive
my desire for more places to go, more bodies to be, this
unbecoming is a motion sickness strung around my ribs,
tightening

my body as an extractive landscape

drown out that fire with your own spit, girl, you are
laden with love of the wildflowers; here my body lies
supine in the forest. from it, i grasp the longing
build skin into desert where i have become
all that has been taken from me. there is
something about this appetite that asks
to give back, as if to open my veins
and let blood cry the creek bed dry. and
with this despair, i still steal what i can
from my own shoulder bones and hips,
we are all stunningly unaware of what it is
we are giving up. my lungs are a passive voice
singing their own song in a heart-held harmony

elevation 9400   38.90494, -120.13516

i am waking on soil
wanting so desperately to write the blood
out of me, but fear keeps running
my pen dry of ink, so instead
i become tire tracks in the august desert
bending rubber against sand, i am
looking for shade, for ease. what taught me
to say my comfort can only be found in clean sheets
in hot water, in scrubbing myself out
of dirt, releasing the silk i keep inside
waiting for myself to grow from the same seed
from which i already tried to sprout.
i am unbound by the terror
of emptying myself of things to say
and ways to explain, all these words
kept inside me in case i need them
next year. if they will fit better
in another notebooks, sewn
with a different leather. take the metaphor
and squeeze every drop of lemon out of it,
every pulling urge for pulp, every tree
and every branch, it grew all of that
just to remind you that words can be written
more than once

i need this wonder to be something i choose

i feel so close to a body of water i do not dare to touch it
you are saying you know everything there is about knowing nothing at all

so i pinch colorado between my index finger and thumb
to be sure all my body has ever wanted to say was stop

i still do not believe i wasn't here yesterday
folding myself into what the tide looks like today, you are

made of sunlight, sweet bread fresh out of your mother's oven
night will always come faster than you want

sleep will steal you away before you have even said goodbye
sign the love letter to the stars with the blade of your father's knife

spit in the page of a book not to defile it
but to love it so much that you become a part of it too

can you want your way into love because i need this wonder
to be something i choose

canvas country

if i learn anything
walking around this lake
i hope it is for each
tree and all the burnt bark
to string the west and east
together, for blisters' willingness
to protect, for the intimacy
of wind through the narrow forest
i can love the discomfort
of toes curled with cold
and the dirt filling the bottom of my sleeping bag
i know the fortune of being okay
with pain, and every time i stand
i wonder how my knees can do this over and over
but i have not yet found that same love
as the words splattered against lines, i say,
life is too short, too long, but never
too much.

is this the same sky i've always known

peanuts left loose in the bottom of an old tent bag,
the smell of sleep and the ache of unwashed hair
i move through the landscape senseless,
too in awe to be anything but my own
each moment is like waking again
the fear that i am haunting myself
out of love, blistering that sky and loving it
too hard, letting my own thoughts be every conversation
i ever hoped to have. i chew through
the grit, gatorade powder thick
against the back of my throat. eyes, greedy or grateful
wildflowers of every color my heart has ever wanted to hold.
i left my words out, the sun took those too. and suddenly
there is the itching feeling of familiarity, of where have i seen this
before, is this the same sky i've always known

wood that doesn't burn, but flowers   *to lila*

will i wake up to realize
i have been writing the same poem
for eleven years now, circling
around the feeling of home, naming it
so many times the definition dissolves
but with every desire to write something
new, i uncover more ways to explain this,
an obsession with the movement, the belief
in the road. if i settle i fear
there will be nothing more to reason with
and i would have to believe
that this is a place to stay, flounder in
blow on smoke and not see it move anywhere but here
i need to feel her eyes as something to see
every morning, like sunlight, like a shift

to day, a meaning i don't have to define
she makes me want to want, she is
skin i never knew i needed, a smile
that will never stop growing, ever, love
has not for a single moment felt like this
wood that sits in the fire and doesn't burn
but flowers, wanders, finds my mind on her
in the forest, at the summit, inside
of every beautiful thing nature has offered
and still she is more. she is the movement
i have run from and the stillness in her voice
that tells me it is okay, this time, to stay.

you can know and still not do; it is the anomaly of
understanding

i am with only my body in the desert, with a thirst
that grows from every empty creekbed and the water i have
i don't think i will drink. my skin dusty with the paper skin
of peanuts, i carry with me my consumption
knees bent in sand. out of a plastic bag, i pour
sweetened pineapple, dried small by sugar, i have
crystallized myself into knowing i cannot
taste it anymore, my own relief found in burying
sustenance, how hard it is to carry everything i will not eat
i dream of a bag light with only necessity and purpled
by the west edges of a paperback novel
spine twisted with a willingness to fit
bear claws on the bark of a tree, a sound drowned
only by words, a world not determined
by the blinking red light of a battery draining,
i sit staring at trees i don't know the name of
wondering why we decided red was the color of stop
i am haunted by ants, trying to figure out why
i protect my belongings from them, the things i brought
into their home. perhaps it is their freedom in movement,
the constant crawl, the inability to be
where i am exactly like them. they are exploring
by means of fear, ripping their way through the smells
of instant coffee and socks still damp
from yesterday's sweat. i am so paralyzed
by words i don't mind how they lick my breakfast,
i am so taken aback by the way the sun hits the mountains
i feel like i could stare forever and still not understand
how the light moves. in afternoons i follow the shade
and shadow, the sun a torment of heat and i spend
the whole day thinking about how the sun is all our warmth and

light and living and still, we have to protect ourselves from her
burns, the fear of the red, the scalloped skin,
maybe today the sun was just too passionate,
we wandered into her dance an uninvited guest
at her party, i am always a guest of this earth and maybe
it was never meant to be a singular house, but
a home, one that i bury my own sustenance in, constantly
trying to protect myself from the wonder, fear
is where we all are born but i am digging
a grave on the ocean's floor just to take it back
where i fear not my life but just my own comfort.
discomfort is only the feeling of want. i am certain i exist
as more than what i crave, maybe someday i will be sand
and i will understand why it shies
from water, why it buries itself deep. for now, i know
only the yearning, and how to dream

to feel my body like it is the entire earth

i want to feel my body so viscerally i breathe it myself
to understand its every corner, take naps in my nailbeds
believe hunger is not greed but a feeling of trust, to read
rupi kaur's *self-pleasure is self-preservation* and unwrap
each inch of skin that has yet to see the daylight.
it is terrifying to make myself homesick for a house
i never had, one i cannot return to, to build my own
with my bones and the grit my legs have learned, experiences
only i have put them through, watch in wonder
as they recover, as *'only to the degree that we expose ourselves
over and over to annihilation can that which is indestructible
in us be found'* pema chodron, the ghost of my mind's
wisdom. i am tattooing my ankles
with the ink of another artist's words, letting them dance
around my knotted toes, to know my want and how
to achieve not a carving but a grounding, i am more
than my body and i am only my body, how long
can i grow and still love myself, i hope it is forever—

veins look like this when they cry

what is this that i am doing
pressing the 8 key so many times that it breaks even
infinity's infinity. today bleeds no self-help
book, the words of someone whose body is built
by love alone. rather, today is a wandering and
a wondering; if this body is actually one i can call mine
or if the day i put it in the dryer, turned the heat on
too high, tumbled it dry for too long, if that was when
i returned it, it became a lost-and-found leftover, or is it
clothing crumpled in my childhood bedroom
while i live across the country and don't
dare to return to that lonely body. winter fingers
and muscles crowned with nothing, movement
across landscapes on legs, the only things left growing
veins look like this when they cry; ribs try
to break themselves out, run a fracture through
the sternum, return itself to my mother, as if to say
i'm not ready for this life yet. my body lives
a contortionist, a panting dog with no control over its tongue
standing up to touch a sky that is only a ceiling

if i could stop the taunting, stop swallowing
hummingbirds just to feel them flap themselves
a circle in my stomach, precondition
and recondition myself, turn destruction
to a trail marked by blue blazes, turn wonder
into a kind of feeding, one that is not mine
but all of ours. i want to no longer be
by myself in this schoolhouse, i am stuffed
between the walls and shadow of a boarding school
bulging against window glass and screen, never
wanting to say that i never stopped this, i

15

never turned off the dryer and i never folded the laundry
and i never put it in drawers, i never even made myself
a room to keep everything left shrunken, and there is still
no home to put me in

as if to return myself to the sea

august   39.17504, -119.90193

my last night in the forest
i recall writing about the moon. this time
it is still too light, the world and all the passengers
awake, setting myself a solstice to make
june and november blend into one so i cannot
tell a difference in anything but words

the tents under the trees quiver with wind
the gentle shuffle of sleeping bag skin
branches and leaves that will never stop waving
i don't think i have ever left the forest alone

now i am parting with the feeling
that life is not meant to be felt always and only
in solitary, supine, i can still be
everything i am with someone else.

a meditation on nature

nature is not the cure, not the medicine,
nature is the pill bottle and the drive to the pharmacy,
nature is the cvv code on the back of a credit card,
nature is the half empty tank of gas,
nature is the side of the car with that one scratch,
nature is the lessening of nausea after vomiting,
nature is falling asleep in the afternoon
nature is the side effects, the tolerance, the reliance,
nature is the acceleration onto the highway,
nature is loving the yellow light,
nature is breaking in the right lane, the slowing down,
nature is the desire,
nature is the way your stomach hurts after laughing too hard,
nature is peeling an orange in the shower,
nature is new hampshire, but not only the good parts,
nature is slamming your finger in the door and loving the pain,
nature is the frozen bag of mangoes to keep the swelling down,
nature is your favorite t-shirt left in the laundry basket,
nature is your middle school notebook you find
        in your childhood closet,
nature is when the candle has been burning for so long
        is has become liquid,
nature is the way that your hiking boots freeze when they're left
        in the cold,
nature is that oddly warm day in february that makes you think
        it is spring,
nature is that disease that only webmd would ever diagnose you with,
nature is the sound the door makes when closed slowly
nature is keeping the baby blanket,
nature is arriving at the airport two hours early
        just to see the planes fly,
nature is when you finally recognize the song playing on the radio,

nature is your fifth grade graduation,
nature is when you find a matching pair of socks in the dryer,
nature is the way the christmas tree looks on new years,
nature is the low battery, the no outlets,
nature is building a fire with wet logs,
nature is not the cure, just the medicine.

every trail marked with longing

to see a lake only in contrast with sky
beauty in the purification of well water
a few too many tides away from here
i am watching smoke brush the leaves
of every tree in the forest, gently
like only a mother could. it is doing all it can
not to hurt. what would it look like

if all these flowers blossomed at once
if they were bright enough to see the yellow a mile up
and still climbing, if wonderland was defined
by the ground it is built upon, rooted,
staring into a blue-smoked sky. i whisper

to hear my own voice, to brighten my eyes
in understanding of a world with destruction
that will not, cannot, destroy anything
beyond what it can repair, blackened trunks
sometimes think themselves green, bark-born, they are
finding what they are to be in fire. even
miles away the burning groans across the landscape

but there is no part of me that can't find awe
in wind blowing, the sweetened smell of sage
drawing sweat-soaked skin with nature's body
and for every cut to seal itself dry, blood lust
heat that is honeycomb, a thousand bees
building their houses in places we have yet to name

every trail is marked with this, the longing
and it takes all my breath not to call it my home
too

call it dirty, i call it me   42.97479, -70.94201

i call it the way my fingers were born
with dragging cuticles and blood stains
i was always meant to wear this
the meaning of constant
calm and rejection. i see
how my arms are bones of feeling
and i was too stuck looking outside
to notice their movement, their dance

i wish for a kind of running
that screams the return, mud miles
in dark blue dusk, along paths
paved with the footprints of others
running home. there is nothing
as bright as the moon's wild touch
and bodies moving silently across land
letting rain be just sweat and wonder

leaving reno, west   39.46764, -120.00310

city limits bound by cigarettes smoke and want
this heat that reminds me of every place
i'll never go, that the same sun
that shines in denver also wakes here—
it's a place too damp to be called a desert
where walmart employees wear sunglasses inside
and ice melts before it is even frozen. every car in neutral, stalling
not daring to move. every strip mall along this boulevard
darkened with air conditioning bills too high to keep the lights on
this gas is cheap because it doesn't fill me up like fuel should
smoke stealing the space between me and my rearview mirror,
whatever is in bleeds its way out. i can drive as fast
as this speedometer goes, and i still can't run it out of me
the heat, the wet

waking the wanderer

water, sweet with sun

feel the exhilaration of sugar, stuck
to the edges of your cheeks, girl, if i had
as much paint on my body as you, i would
become, i would watch it all dry and then
peel myself away to find what's underneath
it is words, then, it is the feeling
the letters evoke. i am no more than
my own pen ink on paper. what i leave
to this world is a language someday
nobody may understand, but they can look
at the pen's movement and know it is passion. i will
keep them wondering how long i can last
following the sun and writing the way it feels

i have spent my entire life growing this

i am writing through every 'can't' to realize it's a 'won't'
like i will lay an iron on my most delicate skin just to see
if i will finally blister, throw metal in the fire to feed it
wishing to clean water with itself, droplets drying
around burnt-up match sticks, a uselessness
that has never meant more. what is it
i am trying to find with this feeling of alone
what else won't i do, cry out, define it, so contorted
inside of the world that distance can only ever be
physical, that no matter my mailing address i will always
sleep next to you. maybe i have been
dreaming myself into the same forest every night
that is why these leaves feel so familiar, because
i have spent my entire life growing them

porchlight butterfly

violet wildflowers beached against the california state line
the sun is sinking wet under the foothills, i am climbing on
to somewhere i have told my map to take me. rocks
so white they look like puddles of snow in july,
heat waves brought by wind and taken by the trees
it is like i am standing on a porch waiting for the love of my life
to come home, and with each switchback
she is that much closer, my thighs dancing their way to dinnertime
this joy dissolves any fear that i am
a waterbottle being emptied on the desert floor. rather
every breath is as it should be—heavy

a forest road pickup truck   39.2259, -120.13660

men's voices, loud and echoing
across miles of water, i am
everything i need and still there is
the slam of keys into an ignition
car doors with more sound
than the zipper of every tent in the forest
and the groan of an engine slipping on socks
these tires doubt themselves. someone is
cursing the metal as it bends, whining
as i pinch my leggings and the dirt
billows out, like aluminum is waiting
for me to leave, so it can scream

to the post office in meyers, california   38.85346, -120.0155

yes, i am trying to buy a one-way train ticket
from the service desk in a post office, pleading
my way into trading coins for the ten miles it would take
to finally get away from myself; i have always
addressed every package wrong, even myself

there were years i would mail myself letters, the joy
in seeing an envelope with my name on it, a full mailbox
like a full belly sick with oil bills and papercuts, how old was i
when i memorized my home address, learning of zipcodes
and their insignificance in every border ever built

when i said i don't want an address, was i saying
i want no letters, no words, no po box number
no catalogs left between the seats of my car

wind on the water

fingers dip themselves in secrecy
and come up empty. you are
desperately trying
to identify a metaphor
that has no meaning. this ship
is only a toy sailboat wrapped in glass. this
lake dreams to have only a coast and no ocean
i am carrying three books
up this mountain, seeing
if i can outline it with my words

all i want is the return

the urge to disconnect comes fast. i am dreaming
about where i wish to be without realizing
i am already there

i'm thinking about how
loneliness didn't feel lonely until i had someone
to love. opportunity is a broken-winged
butterfly that asks to be caught
when all it wants is the return

dusk and dirty

the feet of a child in soft sand
fold themselves down towards the earth
hiding and wishing to be water. i am certain
we all wish to be water. it is
everything; how could i ever decide
between the mountain and the sea
we are all the mountains and we are all the sea

waking the wanderer

waking up with wonder, today
the only one waiting for me is me
i am trying to remember what the sky looks like
when it isn't ombre with smoke
the ants are awake, too, crawling themselves
a circle around my smells

slowly

last night, drunk in flame and dream
i walked myself back to west virginia, the only place
i didn't love the fire, where thick air didn't make me
feel any fuller and wanted nothing more
than to spit in my bloody embers

and it never melts, in summer's county
there are cards on the bedside table, cots contained
in bedframe imagination. spiders that crawl above
the ceiling rafters, smoke when you turn on the faucet
and again, you ask for escape, for dirt
that curls itself into a tree, for the black shape of love
to shake itself through you, to light a candle
with your own tongue

but the letting go, the slipping into sleep,
socks left by the foot of your bed, you wake and wonder
whether your mind burnt here or there, nowhere
and no water, not tonight

morning born

i am scared of the last sip of coffee
where the dirt settles and tells me to drink
where an empty cup shows me a reflection
of what i have consumed, what
lives inside me now is the part
oftentimes leftover. with every ounce
i am swallowing purity to equal my dirt
and wringing my hands like they are the rags i made wet
i think under morning starlight is the only place beans and rice
have ever tasted this good, where i don't mind
drinking the last sip of coffee while it's still hot and
nowhere close to cold

loneliness can look like this

i have been holding
on to strangers'
words, trying to make them
mean more than they do
walking slow in
hopes that someone will
catch up and tell me
it is okay, you can
do this, i know it

sandcastle landscape

there were so many faces at south lake tahoe
beach, i burnt my feet in sand just staring
at the water between them, its cloudy fog, restlessness
like the waves want to stay still and watch these mountains
like i can. i want to feel it beyond
the selfish wetting of a sweaty body
and leaving my backpack in the sand. trying to see sand
as its own sandcastle, asking itself for the morphing,
loving the wounds of their touch. perhaps it is
jealousy, the humiliation of wanting
my own, a family that likes umbrellas
but likes the sun more, a bathing suit beyond
running shorts, dirty for a week.
and as soon as i am there, i want myself away
tucked into woods with only the faces of trees
as company

tell me about the caldor fire while i wish the trees well

it is like walking into a ghost forest, a grave
even the footsteps plead silence, as if
crushing another black branch to flat ash
is what makes it die. the trees still standing
are still perishing, are still
there are no mosquitoes, no squirrels
the only sound is my own breath, i
quiet every noise, solemn hatred for the wind
and the matches, and the gun
to shoot back at itself, bring fire inside
and leave the forest be. this
community unleashed and evacuated
to places where smoke doesn't fill the holes
but perhaps the sea, and they leave but
never return, the coffeeshop on the corner
burying its beans in fury and fear
there are no people; we have too much
and too much burnt. the return to
the burn scars is whistling in open air
emptiness and longing and the feeling
of walking on hot rocks in the california sun
with no shoes, just blisters, and it's not a good burn.
it is the terror that keeps you going. it is.

and the water screams back

i lay my hand on pebbles warm with morning sun
if a lake can have a coast, this is it. there is
nothing to hear but breath and echo
hikers padding along the edge, the only
restlessness is a hunger for water, this blue
that reflects sky has a needing to be near
haunting the sunlight by living in its shadow
this landlocked ocean and forest neighbor; it is cracked open
and wondering which direction to go, which tide
to swim towards, what do i do with this loneliness, i am
looking not for love but for the liminal. each tree
the wrong one to cut down—what i have learned
from this ocean blood is that a sea can be
anything at all, my own spit even. am i just saying
words that have already been said? can enough
be written about the water if every moment in front of it is new

madness

i am in love with the way i can
make myself drunk on cowboy coffee and granola bars

the recentering

for the hours i spent trying to find a difference
in oceans

moving the center of a map, westward
so exit 204 is not a destination, just
a truckstop on the way through. this ocean is always
split by perspectives; we name it based
on where we are, when the ocean never stops
touching itself. what we see is water, nothing i have
ever wanted more than to make it all one

wonderland

how could a whole day be gone? me longing
for more time in the woods, always just
yesterday. i, tired like greasy hair, wound myself
to braids, cooked hot coffee over a camping stove
and forgot about it until it was cold. here
i am less than my own doubt and more
than any sickness i dare to wrap my mind around
i can already sense deep sadness in the leaving

bound to be ugly

if i am what i was

conscious of self, i am
in dirty clothes, soaked so many times
with sweat, they crease themselves clean
it did not feel so odd, until i was here
the urge to curl away alone and fierce
but this town has a safety in it
where i string myself along the treeline
go to a restaurant with only me
just to order the macaroni and cheese without the cheese
i cannot pin down the chaos, and how it startles
the softness and quiet of the lake
a pier so long you doubt it even connects to land or sea
i am chewing my fingernails in anticipation of bread
for balsamic olive oil, and
the next morning, waking to a car alarm
is like a wildfire whisking me out of my tent

denver

i am like every blade of grass growing
in the sidewalk cracks and bending against
the curb. it only makes sense when plastered
against the rubbing of the road

i want semblance like i want it to be thursday
consistency a dependent variable fighting against the feeling of
my backpack doesn't feel like mine yet
so i clean my car with the red dirt of a colorado forest road
waking myself up on sand beside a stream in utah
wondering what it will take for my legs to run away today

when i see denver, i think of seven months plus
a few days in late may and early june, a week
in august. i make it my own flyover state
i make the road a scattering of coffeeshops
along borders bound by mountains, to listen
not to myself, but to the regulars, who order
their latte the same every morning, how they know
the name of the barista and i barely know
the name of this town.

bound to be ugly

someone tell me how the sun moves through the canyon
so i can walk along its edge, exchange a run in the rain
for a flash flood, finally willing the cold to come
and i never thought it would, rather
my refrigerator skin unplugged from the socket
of digestion, for the incision to scissor itself into
the blunt knife of hope, wondering if i could know
my stomach like i know the slickrock
it's bound to be ugly, this unfolding, not
shade or sage. i am a lizard running
from my own shadow. to slow this life down
is not to forget, but it is certainly not to remember
i'm stuck in moab thinking that meaning
is defined by the meaningless, outlined
by its own lack. if i loved my body
like i loved the thought of leaving, perhaps
i would have become entirely forest, unrooting,
tucked behind all that is hidden, stealing glass
from the desert and waiting for it to learn
how to see again, how to touch its own muscles
just to try to repair, how to be unbroken, how to reach
out and touch childhood like the first time
you saw your reflection in a bathroom mirror
do you remember your first day of school
that is how the canyons feel every morning before they learn
the movings of the sun

desolate, i'm supposed to be alone

wilderness, but only in theory
never in practice, barely enough
to let myself believe i am
out here, finally hiking the land
i never thought myself well enough
to do, at least not in this lifetime

mirror mountain

watching my reflection in the bottom of a glass
is the first time i have seen my face
in six days, since my last bathroom mirror
and not even a gas station, but a cafe
with $8 cups of coffee. i have been watching
my body every day now to ensure
it is not growing anything but grit
to make sure my pants get bigger
so i can stretch them with the sun
and my waist gets smaller so my frame
is not so heavy to carry. i could
get rid of these three notebooks and keep my body
but i am not as good at skin as i am with words
my hair bleached lighter by sun, my feet
dirtier with blisters. every day, another
day to prove myself enough, a strength
that only comes with breath

when i become vain, i become

all i want is to walk around you, laugh you
to the shore and leave my handprints in wet sand
for gravity to eat. this is all i've ever wanted
to be in this place, though all morning my mind
convinced me my body too ugly for even nature to love
angry at its clumsiness, with no acknowledgement
of all the work it has done to get here.
i like my skin better like this, in the dirt. i don't
care about its shape until suddenly i do. my
shadow a line not of the thinness my city body
wanted. how dare i use the undergrown and overtold water
for *this,* to shrink

do you have any idea who you are not

i was in eighth grade when i wore my first pride shirt
and was told to take it off. *it was for my own
safety*, the guidance counselor said, *when you are
a little older, you can make that decision*

small town whispers and PTA meetings ripe
and absent of the parents of the children who dared to
climb in the monkey bars past fourth grade, all at once
they saw me taking too many shots at a gay bar in boston
drunk on the idea that life could be this beautiful

but never leaving my parents' house, they saw me
letting my body grow soft and fleshy and using it
for nothing. i was a student
labeled studious but i must be careful not to study
the wrong things. a masquerade game
of disguise, the only girl in a row of trumpets, nothing
louder than the shame that i would never be the girl
to play the flute, behind an instrument
i could scream my identity anywhere without holding
all it meant and all it could mean, for me

i can hear the highway from the hills

my obsession with cars grows the farther i get from the highway

it feels like i have been waiting years
to throw this old warm bottle of mountain dew
in the backseat of a sudan, to let liquid wetten itself
and claim to be no more than flat wheels

certain and poised that you are
whatever car you drive, i am always tied
between the yellow light and the yellow line
crossing pavement to get to trail, watching
evening turn headlights brighter each hour, wondering
who lives here, in the space that moves between

and i sat listening to traffic in dirt and stain
in anticipation of the next gas station
lemonade, the only place beyond the trails
open all hours of day and night

desert body

love is an analogy i have not tangled myself in
before this year i could not have even tried
i wake up every day and know the desert is safer
but not as radiant as her presence. how fear and love
can sometimes feel the same

do you want to know, or not

this truth is the wind that carries smoke
across mountain ridges. in it, i see
losing my running shoes under a bed that's not mine
putting away the mirror skin i have sculpted
and falling too hard, always,
at the punch line of a joke. this is funny,
if i can explain it. i am
following actions that will make nobody laugh
except the part of me that fears the wonder

words i cannot erase but can define

i want to write words i cannot erase
any question i'm asked where the answer is
i love woman, peel back the sticky side of every stamp
to outline where gender turns to woman, where love becomes
more than friendship

when the grocery store shelves
are taller than the highest mountain i've submitted
the words eating disorder don't need to be
defined, though i wish i could
tangle some vowels to include recovery, to
include work and what happens beneath when
the gas station doesn't have any granola bars
for my physiatrist to understand i am not a lesbian
i am gay, and yes, how i identify myself is a definition
made up entirely by me

wreck it, make it art, finally

i am knitting together every thread in the house
trying to find the part where i meet myself

it is long overdue, this library return date used only for shelving

i can check to make sure all my bones are there
but i don't remember where they go. all i know

is the night sky is actually just the ending of your favorite song
and sunrise—not time zones—is what breaks up this earth

i am stuck in a video game glitch, forever remembering
the first time a comic strip was aminated into a film

when movement became art, stretching itself
across every shoot and up every ladder, mushroom

your mind to see the grand canyon from every planet
but ours. when i look at my body i think of every valley

i've ever thrown a pebble down into, skipping rocks
across algae water just to let them sink. i find myself

and my skin scotch-taped between canyon ledges
the confluence of the colorado and the rio grande

beneath, waiting for its chance to taste what loneliness looks like

doubt dumb

doubt rings a little doorbell in my soul, opens
a deck of tarot cards at dusk
in the san juan mountains, august,
goddess of doubt, make me
an anthill of yeasted hope caught
fire, no flame

female, 21, green eyes

neither sight or sound
fear flies straight towards sunburnt skin
reminds me what red can do,
i've never seen a helicopter land on a ridgeline
until today. i hope it scared
the bears crawling these woods as much
as it shook me. i forget which state i am in
when i see search and rescue, when
every nail is patched black with dirt
i think i may have left my fingerprints
in the stream between lakes, certain
no one will find me. i have become so good
at burying my bones and setting fire against them

what can i say

except you are going to give up before me
i am playing with dice on a coffee-stained foldout table
running through my odds and evens, fingering
the spines of the months in-between
the terrifying fleeting thought *what if i was never
actually in recovery?* what does empowerment mean
if i don't speak the language

i listen to music because it is the space between
the sickness, weeks in parenthesis, the *it was all good*
except for this one flash flood in durango
where even the subarus got stuck in the mud
where i spent the loveliest part of the day in a parking lot
trying to figure out how to fix a broken radio

i sleep better on the ground than i do in a bed, my back
meant to hold itself against rocks. i read for so long
it is morning again, sing myself a ballad away,
only on the highway i remember recovery, playing
back memory loops of *did i eat that day*
i am a built-in distraction running the batteries out
an empty gas tank in the desert, backstage
in my own life until i stop
going over and over in my head about if
my body will give up before me. if i will
run it to the ground like the cars in the shop

moments in motion

i really thought nevada didn't look like this
i really thought i didn't look like this, sound like this
splitting an entire lake in two, willing
state lines to dance on moving tides. gold light
of the east side, dried eyes in sand-burnt skin

a poem is never finished and never unfinished

it is here i will meet myself

the hunter

to write about a person is to write about a place i know too well,
like i'll never forget your body's shape, that untraceable spine,
that number in handprint paint on nobody's new mailbox.
my wonder, then, is nothing if mountain peaks don't look
like the beaks of birds who flew too high and fell. you are leaving words
in my veins, as coiled genes, every sound goodbye dares to let itself feel,
suddenly all i can picture is the shadow in your favorite photograph

i'm sitting in the library studying magazine covers,
thinking about the people who wake up and aren't me.
how i will never know what that feels like. how can i
capture a selflessness without separating me from me,
without burying myself in my own ashes and striking another
match. it is horrifying how many things i will never learn,
the words i will never write all the things i have seen
just to not see again
were the last words i spoke to my first grade teacher goodbye

inside, i breathe to the sound winter coats make when they move
like the down of that baby bird is life itself,
like a jacket holds enough heat to start a slowing heartbeat.
i remember winter only as it's opposite; i swear to god it is bones
bending themselves, make me believe that pain is weakness
leaving the body, and here, i draw myself
a venn diagram just to see where our fingertips meet
if there was a cure to this disease
the forgetting, we would have found it years ago

clay boy

silly boy, trying to carve yourself out of clay and a toothpick
don't you know you're only the negative space shadow and shade
this bird flew its nest only when it found another
animal to be. to me
your art easel way will never have lines to color in
rather, my mother is on the phone reminding you
that toothpicks should only be used to see if the cake is cooked
through, not some mirror test, not in the basement
of a philadelphia apartment complex
nothing rises there. you are moving
the metronome between daughter and son, suddenly
having the knowing the pencil writes from both ends
but not yet realizing the eraser doesn't come back
the butanol of a bent sharpie, crossing
me out, a permanent line over ~~SISTER~~
warping 2010 ten years so fast my own memory film
skips ahead, the curtain draws back, your headshot shows
flannel buttoned all the way to the top. the phone never
stops, for you, its ring is a fire alarm out of batteries
where everyone is still looking for the smoke. for you
my mother rebuilds the nest out of every animal
you could ever wish to be, and it is still not enough
in this gallery, the one shaped by my own miles
outlined on an atlas, you are
an honorable mention, but one i will still remember
years after visiting every art museum in paris
you, i will still never forget

if only you knew the answers to all my questions; if only i believed them

i am sitting on the curb, the voices of hikers just an echo of earth's walls
when a woman in sunglasses asks me if i believe in god
squinting down at me, dissecting what has already been pulled apart
is my answer, something that should be retracted, extracted, or,
how do i,   do i even tell her   no

she says she is a jehovah's witness, poses a question

 is the world getting worse?

                                                  yes.   i have to answer

why does god want us to suffer? something better is coming!
it's coming so soon! god asks us to wait

she hands me a bent pamphlet out of her pocket
as if she has been waiting
for exactly this moment, exactly me to tell this story, this truth to.
i am wondering if i, sitting on pavement with candy in my hands,
dirt on my face and my legs, in my hair; do i
look like who she is looking for?
do i need saving? i am wondering if my face says help me.

she asks

if i have met a jehovah's witness and

i say   no

though my grandfather on my father's side became one
and sent back christmas presents to the return address

and i know of the women who hand out pocket bibles
on the street corner in new hampshire, waving their words
for us to come catch

                              no? no? then i really must explain.

and while she talks i recall my own god,
who only lives below the mason-dixon line
i am too tired from walking through the desert
to tell her all the reasons in my head
why god is not real, but from the moment
she asks me if i believe in god
she is not asking, but

telling me. i must say   yes yes   please, of course

i read every night the words from a poetry book
and she reads the bible. i memorize mile markers
and the sun's shadow between my legs
while she eats lines from a hardcover book
that can be printed in every size, as if made
just for everyone looking to hold it

who prints the bible, anyway

my belongings are splayed out on the sidewalk
as if i have everything i need
except
my own god

i believe in wonder,   in desert!

in dry land that begs to be seen

63

i have begun to believe in living

the next morning, i sit in my own sweat to open the pamphlet.
i have never felt paper

　　　　　so light, so unacknowledged

and i am not the crying woman on the front, finally
there is a mailing address for new york, a QR code
and a quote that says, in cursive

in the meantime god tenderly comforts
those who sincerely look for him
those who sincerely look for him, those who sincerely look

for home, i am waning off, not laughter but sadness knowing there are
people
who think i am going to hell,
though i never asked her if this god sent the gay people to hell,
but i imagine probably,　　　　　yes

if there was more in me than doubt
i would read that pamphlet instead of poetry,
translation after translation

and still i didn't know
the difference between catholicism and jehovah's witness
eighteen years of sundays in an episcopal church,
 i must have worked really hard
to not listen to any of it
i told the woman at the trailhead

　　　　　　　　　i used to go to church

she said
she stopped going to church at my age too
but found it again, and   i thought

i have found so much more wonder than god

i have found

mountains built entirely on courage, every shade
of love that dares to climb it, and joy
that comes from finding the only stream
in a 30 mile stretch of dry land

does she know how much power, how many gods there are
on this trail alone
how i have been a witness to suffering and it has

survived me, guided me

towards a belief so strong i am learning to love myself
like i am the entire earth

i might have already passed my best day
the promised land could already be here, in these trees
no god is saving anything for us
and i will spend the rest of my life
believing in loving the girl who holds my sweaty hand
and building back every tree i have caused to burn

is it time now, to give up, i mean

i am in massachusetts
wondering how my own love can be someone else's
pain

my childhood bedroom is a scab i have picked to blood
a waterbottle with a leak, a cooler of melted ice
and i did that, to you. to her. i am stuck in the way
not of being motionless, but of being in too much
motion, being in too much flight without
wings or bird-bones. i don't want stability
i want to stand on stilts in the wind and wait
for something to hold onto

i wake up today only to write, to try
to make sense of it all in lowercase
buttons of words, my own thoughts
filling someone else's head. and near dawn
i remember houses only as they do not look
like mine, as my parents roam
the world i worked so hard to call my own
as massachusetts bleeds colorado mountain
money, a shifting, i was never ready for

what do i say to myself the nights
when my choices make my mother cry

bedroom body

all that is left there is my childhood
bed and bookcase and the sound
of my grandmother's voice the first time
i drove by myself to the red house, latching
a seatbelt, tight around growing up

i have scraps of stories in journals left
in a doorless closet, collections of feelings
a few too many pencils with no tip
thinking this is where the pain bleeds out
not in the lyrics of someone else's song, but in my own
body, to feel my bedroom body like it has never slept

the epitome of the staircase—weight exactly
the depth of this rapid fear
to prove to myself these bruises weren't given by me
i'm sorry i loved you too hard
and forgot what the childhood, the pictures, tell

they tell us all cold on the beach

praise the moment when "we're doing all we can"
is not enough, but not not enough to make me leave
not everybody's family is built on fear. when i found this
out, i spent hours at the library reading my way
into someone else's dream. and i wished for a sister

like i wished to eat only the popcorn's old maids
like i wished for her to go too far, like sterile
and skeptic doctors, degrees to give me a new room
give me a reason to never miss the return

my mother's garden

she started growing vegetables the year we moved out
called to tell me about the tomato plants
about the sweetness of the first one to be ripe
the herbs flourishing when i was not there
to eat them straight off the stem
and the balloon flowers were never popped
they just opened when it was time
cody would trample through the garden, paws
on growing petals, in the spring
when they first widened their eyes, while
our bare feet, white with cold, slipped around
on melting snow. these are stills, no life
or movement to the colors now, just the hard frame
of old photographs, one after another
on the living room table; snow that always stays

making the forest a home   44.01130, -71.35329

carving branches with my fingernails, combing
my hair with every piece of dry bark i find

the woods i grew up in: those trees
with perpetual dew neatly placed on each leaf
a forest floor hiding its own liveliness, death threat and wet
remember what a fallen tree trunk could become for us
summer running across moss in the rain, cobwebs in our eyelashes
and dirt on the pads of our feet. the last time we scraped our shins
on the rock face, i left blood behind and
never came back for it. perhaps that is
why now i cannot leave it be

you make the woods a strip mall shopping center
i race through, waiting in a checkout line
with no items to buy but as much cheap wood as i dare carry
home, a magazine only with pictures
of houses high in trees, soiled with knowledge,
every nail hammered into glass that never stops
shattering

i want to be able to run through every trail
and not feel any of it. no matter how damp the forest
i always leave more thirsty. when moving wasn't enough
to stitch every handheld wound, i started laying
on rocks heavy with sun, panting from the exhaustion
of stopping, guilt leaving dead pine needles in the shade
of every tree. there was a solace in the destruction, a madness
of being, my inability to accept my own sweat leaving me
blind at nightfall, still searching for the right moss to uproot
i blame it on your absence sometimes; you took my childhood
because you couldn't have yours, but you gave me the woods

when we were still kids, and still have not forgiven me
for keeping them.

tell me all your secrets, i'll tell you what i know

how do you say his name
the way it swarms around in your mouth
spits itself on skin, threatens life
to make you look, screams for rescue
but will not take any raft in the open ocean, tell me
how you look through photos and cross out curls
let spring always reverse itself into winter; you
cry more at his cuts than my tears. there is the trust
i will never get back that you give him every day.

the child of guilt and deviance

i emptied my heart into my own safety
a knot only i can undo, it is like
falling without letting go, giving myself
everything i never knew i could give
shame grows mold on this, smells
like something kicked under the bed
the thought everyone thinks but nobody says
disappointment is my truth, it is
my breath. expectations line up, dominoes
bolted to a plastic ground, make up my own
language to put words to this feeling,
the child of guilt and deviance

west virginia moon and smoke   37.68527, -80.71866

every time i see smoke like this
it is west virginia; it is the deep august moisture
only fire can run through. the room
where i wait outside the kitchen window
for my half scoop of granola. the swing
outside where my mother picks me up
sixty days too late, cradling itself ever so slightly
against air so still a whisper could move it

west virginia was so wet with thunderclouds
i ran around the mansion jailhouse
to create rain myself, to make me go inside
to see a bathroom door that is actually a curtain
to rinse my body dirty, a god that maybe
if i prayed to, or wore enough cardigans
would claim me cured and let me go

claim me cured and let me go, i cried
always and always i cried into open air
if there was any marker of depression
it was my entire body, dry. so what i worked on
all those months south, is the understanding
that this is not a john denver song—john denver
must have been in colorado when he wrote
about west virginia—there are no country roads
i have ever met that look like this

cloth hunger

this want is defined only by what it is not
brain-blind and injured; a side of stitches
running too straight to be anything but
drawn-on sharpie against a rag doll's belly
a marker bleeding red on swollen cloth.

"i want" is a phrase bound by its own greed
its own plastic puzzle and cellophane wrapped
toy store aisle, wanting to want with eyes alone
a mouth that curtains its words and willingness
no lace, no silk, no size chosen up or down. i fit
myself into the clothes as the clothes don't
fit themselves into me. i leave myself
only hand-me-downs

with crayola i dare to sketch a barbie
into a brat—me, but a doll accessorized by pink
and black—the only greed i can ever have
is one inked with words, bound by heaviness
and the deep isolation and wonder of
reading every story i wish to twist myself into

girlhood is greed in itself. sometimes, perhaps
the expansion of one's body is a series of expectations of
how much weight should i gain during puberty? because
life like this is measured by percentiles, by
where do i fall in comparison to every other eleven year old
it's just not right to be bigger than my thirteen year old sister
but still i am sitting in the backseat writing myself a script
how to tell my mother my clothes are getting too small
and i learned that deserving takes time; i squeezed
too much from those early years, building my belief

that i am no more than the sum of my consumption. those were
the years the american girl doll catalog played a pillow
for all the clothes i would never ask for

petal project   38.57355, -109.54568

library petal project: where we bring
flowers and let them grow from the pages
of our favorite stories. each

bookshelf carries all the same words
in a different order, a deepened hole
of assonance in an air conditioned room

we escape here for clean bathrooms and
water fountains, and the dog-eared pages
of every memoir we've never read

for the novels we have written in our head
all displayed into oneness on someone
else's pages; when i walk i speak

to myself and i stamp my stories with my eyes
only, i don't dare open this backpack
for anyone. i am the hardcover too

expensive to buy, too heavy to bring with you,
too new to really understand. so in moab
in durango, in colorado springs, in denver

i bury my roots in the public floors
in the quiet room, in the teens' corner,
in the children's books, in the space between
every book in the library

dreaming myself back to boston

my mother is unwrapping tinfoil cheese at dusk
with knives in the drawer taped closed that my brother would go to
when he started to believe that leaving his body was
the only thing that would keep us loving him

between slices of cheddar, we are a pencil point away

      waiting for the next episode of answers
the credits of a film made only of screams. no one is

recognizable; i am lamplight, backlight, waiting to shatter

and when the camera crew arrives on the front lawn
all they can think is *look how messed up this is*
her father holds the landline but never calls the police

      it would be years before they dared call
      law enforcement on their own child. what a feeling
      it must be, for those buttons to seem a rescue

 a philadelphia apartment and every hospital bed in the city, empty

every morning, i am more certain that i made this up
in my own mind; i am always halfway through
a novel's best chapter when the story ends. it is a power
outage

that is exactly how it felt

what is more a luxury than seeing
your own blood, conscious; to feel
what is alive in you and let it heal
we open wounds to see if pain
feels the same every time and
i am learning it does not

not one of these words is abuse, but all of them
keep me tethered to a child, shelling herself
with a belief that whatever smells like love
always tastes likes naming herself with a death dance
where more life was no prize

you told me bruises are the blood that cannot let go
and there i was, covered in them, little gold star
stickers not saying strength, but dull
weakness, how dare my body show this
hurt, i am a machine stuck and spinning

a gradual incline so gentle it will never break you
does not feel like an incline at all

do you know the feeling of heat so violent
it makes your veins stand on their tiptoes
and scream for release, that is exactly how it felt

the bug house

porcupine quills dare bare feet to dance
on mangled grass, blueberry bushes,
feeding the bears and our purple mouths, sour
until July; we are sticky with the urge to pick
the unripe berries. flowers grow
through the cracks in a well; i am wonderland
in a petal-filled place, in the green and growing
humidity sticks bugs to cheeks and dew to leaves
this world a natural watering can, days framed
by jumping into daylight and waiting for the sun
to crack open. fill its waterfall skin and our glee
as a rope swing leans back and forth against
the groaning of an old tree. the mosquitoes at night
are hungry, so hungry they hum their own song
and ask us, *please, sing along, see me*
for one moment as more than a whine
but we light citronella candles, our own gate
and fence to a space we claim as ours.
that one night: fireworks moving with stars
where a wild field filled briefly with smoke and
we loved it all, the toasting, to colors so unlike
and unaware of daytime flowers, finally
retreating through glass doors only when the bugs drive us
indoors, where the whole room echoes with laughter
and love, more love, than i have ever seen yet
willing, daring, to take up a single space
at morning, the tiles' floors grow warm from
their position in the sun's rising, and here i drink
cranberry juice the color of rose petals in the desert
and a warm blueberry muffin, baked fresh from
yesterday's flour, heated in that microwave
that only works half the days, and it is

the best thing i have tasted since i learned
how to grow my own roots somewhere else
i return to see the first mountain i climbed
still dusted with those same trees. you could have
measured my height on their bark, seen me
grow with them, not forget the rocks that seemed
like boulders, like wandering hands and feet
grasping for a place i knew would be the moon
and at the top, we see our own growing place
a summit where you can count the stars
and the ponds, the glorious lapping waves on shadow sand
where you can write forever and never touch it all
pints of ice cream filled so full they melt
in our palms, sticky and wonderous
with sugar, maybe, a picnic table with those
red and white checkers, a line in the sun, or
the drive home, containers of ice cream on the floor
by the air conditioning on high. i could write
about pasta with basil pesto from your garden, the sound
of dishes as we talk at the table, as the lights
are flipped on, as the darkening sky tiptoes in
where i always know which bed is mine
as footsteps creak on old hallway floor
as i sleep
as i write

it is here i will meet myself

i fight the dirt along the creases of my palm
lake water dreaming to make it clear. it is
here where the perfection wanes
this place is as close to perfect as anything can be

sunscreen smell and the little bugs
that drop themselves in the lukewarm cup
of cowboy coffee, the reason i stay is
a pot boiled burnt with rice and beans
the lasting taste of fire the rest of the month
and to remember that night

there is nowhere that my body has been forgivable
except for here. where sweat is gratitude
i am thankful for every bit of water i am allowed to see
the taste of town still offers me love
in bedsheets and mirrors and the making sure
my tan lines measure the same in the sun's shadow. but i am

a mirror mountain, so i keep myself
humbled by trees and daring to edge the cliffs
to the sky, driving my own life
back towards itself. it is here i will meet myself
for the first time since i was ten years old

writing to the rim   39.16304, -120.14313

the part i remember most is the leaving
writing a series of goodbyes that
even my hands are afraid to read. can i
return my words and ask again

every time i wonder if it is freedom, the unlatching
i come to a conclusion that anything can be
freedom if i continue to think it exactly enough.

the ink in this notebook feels so real i stutter
even in poetry, push myself into the permanence
of believing i am every memory that i document
with my hands, not a photograph or the film i ruined

i am certain i will never touch something as real
as these paper pages, keep me glued to remembering
the leaving, holding the series of goodbyes
and writing to the rim

as if to return myself to the sea

notes

To feel my body like it is the entire earth is a poem inspired by the self-love, self-acceptance, and self-awareness of Rupi Kaur's *Home Body*. This poem also includes a quote by Pema Chödrön, which I first discovered and fell in love with, in Andrea Gibson's *Angels of the Get-Through*.

Wreck it, make it art, finally is a poem whose lines were inspired by a single line of Andrea Gibson's *Jellyfish*. In this poem, they write, "a doctor once told me i feel too much, i said, so does god, thats why you can see the grand canyon from the moon."

The poem *what can i say* is named after Brandi Carlile's song "What Can I Say." Her music and beautiful lyrics have been incredibly influential throughout my writing process.

My body as an extractive landscape is a poem that was originally inspired by a Southwest Studies class I took at Colorado College where we explored the ways in which the southwest region of the U.S. is seen as extractive.

A forest road pickup truck is a poem written at Watson Lake Campground while hiking the Tahoe Rim Trail. Shortly before I stayed at this campground, there was a snowmobile accident in Watson Lake, making the water dangerous to drink.

Dusk and dirty is loosely inspired by Ingrid Michaelson's song "mountain and the sea."

Sandcastle landscape was written during my 170-mile thru-hike on the Tahoe Rim Trail, where I stopped in South Lake Tahoe to feel the water of Lake Tahoe for the first time.

Tell me about the caldor fire while i wish the trees well is a poem dedicated to the parts of the forests and the mountains destroyed by the Caldor Fire of 2021. The Tahoe Rim Trail passes through sections of the forests that were burned. The community is still recovering from this devastating wildfire.

If i am what i was is a poem written about my experience in Tahoe City, California.

the growing place

where i can thinking myself water : Come Home by We Are the Guests

the only body left dancing : Homerun Hitter by Greyson Chance

as if to return myself to the sea : Downpour by Brandi Carlile

my body as an extractive landscape : Look Up Child by Lauren Diagle

elevation 9400 : the author by Luz

i need this wonder to be something i choose : Renaissance Man by Sidney Bird

canvas country : The Tide by The Lonely Heartstring Band

is this the same sky i've always known : Daze by The National Parks

wood that doesn't burn, but flowers : Real Peach by Henry Jamison

you can know and still not do; it is the anomaly of understanding : That Wasn't Me by Brandi Carlile

to feel my body like it is the entire earth : This Body by Hello Saferide

veins look like this when they cry : Glamour Child by Moonrise Nation

august : august by Taylor Swift

a meditation on nature : Sunset Lover by Petit Biscuit

every trail marked with longing : Dreamland by Glass Animals

call it dirty, i call it me : Stick Season by Noah Kahan

leaving reno, west : City of Angels by Em Beihold

waking the wanderer

water, sweet with sun : Better Days by Birdtalker

i have spent my entire life growing this :
Comes and Goes (In Waves) by Greg Laswell

porchlight butterfly : California by Chappell Roan

a forest road pickup truck : Thunder Road by Bruce Springsteen

to the post office in meyers, california : Mess by Noah Kahan

wind on the water : Great Divide by Ira Wolf

all i want is the return : The Joke by Brandi Carlile

dusk and dirty : Cosmic Love by Florence + The Machine

waking the wanderer : World Spins Madly On by The Weepies

morning born : Appalachian Wine by eleventyseven

loneliness can look like this : Passenger by Noah Kahan

sandcastle landscape : when the water meets the mountains by Lewis Watson

tell me about the caldor fire while i wish the trees well :
Turn to Stone by Ingrid Michaelson

and the water screams back : Box of Stones by Benjamin Francis Leftwich

madness : Feel Alive by Katie Herzig

the recentering : Pictures on a Wall by Ira Wolf

wonderland : Stubborn Love by The Lumineers

bound to be ugly

if i am what i was : Wind & Anchor by The National Parks

denver : Sleep On The Floor by The Lumineers

bound to be ugly : Keeping Your Head Up by Birdy

desolate, i'm supposed to be alone : You've Got It by Blsng

mirror mountain : Only Ticket Home by Gavin James

when i become vain, i become : In My Bones by 76th Street

do you have any idea who you are not :
Jacob from the Bible by Jake Wesley Rogers

i can hear the highway from the hills : Highway Honey by LULLANAS

desert body : The Ballad by We Are the Guests

do you want to know, or not : Hallucinogenics by Matt Maeson

words i cannot erase but can define : Easy, Love by Tom West

wreck it, make it art, finally : Vital by Connor McCoy

doubt dumb : Tomorrow by Miner

female, 21, green eyes : I'm Still Trying by Matthew Fowler

what can i say : What Can I Say by Brandi Carlile

moments in motion : Let's See What The Night Can Do by Jason Mraz

it is here i will meet myself

the hunter : i'll die anyway by girl in red

clay boy : No Hard Feelings by The Avett Brothers

if only you knew the answers to all my questions; if only i believed them :
All Too Well (10 Minute Version) by Taylor swift

is it time now, to give up, i mean : You're On Your Own, Kid by Taylor Swift

bedroom body : Northern Attitude by Noah Kahan

my mother's garden : The Mother by Brandi Carlile

making the forest a home : Homesick by Noah Kahan

tell me all your secrets, i'll tell you what i know :
House a Habit by We Are the Guests

the child of guilt and deviance : Dirty Old Town by Craig Cardiff

west virginia moon and smoke : House of Spirits by Allman Brown

cloth hunger : Girl in Calico by Tow'rs

petal project : If You Could Read My Mind by Gordon Lightfoot

dreaming myself back to boston : Family Line by Conan Gray

that is exactly how it felt : Call In The Morning by The Greeting Committee

the bug house : The View Between Villages by Noah Kahan

it is here i will meet myself :
It's a Longer Road to California Than I Thought by The Wind and The Wave

writing to the rim : Rocky Mountain High by John Denver

acknowledgments

Thank you:

to my partner, Lila, for her strength, beauty, and kindness.

to my family in Massachusetts for raising me to love books and supporting me through every passion I have ever had.

to my incredible editor, Flor Ana, and Indie Earth Publishing, the place where my poetry found a home.

to the Colorado College English Department for the continued support and opportunities for learning they offer to me.

to Alli, my brilliant and talented cover artist and friend.

to Dot Devota, for always encouraging my poetry and teaching me how to write fearlessly.

to my best friend, Grace, whose love for adventure has taught me to find courage in my writing.

to Lindsey and Nitya, for helping me hike the 170 miles around Lake Tahoe.

to my grandmother, and her ability to find the beauty in everything.

to Finn, and all the words we have written together.

to the people in my life who have never given up on me.

to everyone who believes that poetry can heal.

to the desert for giving me something to fear, and the mountains for giving me something to wonder at.

to the readers, whose eyes have washed over this tide of poems, thank you.

about the author

© Sam Yolles

Kristen Richards is a poet based in Colorado Springs currently working towards a BA in Creative Writing at Colorado College. Raised in Massachusetts, Kristen attended Phillips Exeter Academy in New Hampshire before moving west where she fell deeply in love with the mountainous landscapes of Colorado. Her work has previously been published in the *Leviathan*, *The Elevation Review*, and *Flossy Lit Magazine*, and her poem *(self)love notes* was also published in *GLOW: Self-Care Poetry for the Soul*. As if to return myself to the sea is her first poetry collection. She loves creating poetry outdoors, usually accompanied by the sunrise, an oat milk latte, and Mary Oliver's poem *Wild Geese*.

Connect with Kristen on Instagram:

@kristenrichardspoetry

ABOUT THE PUBLISHER

Indie Earth Publishing is an independent,
author-first co-publishing company based in Miami, FL, dedicated to
giving writers the creative freedom they deserve when publishing their
poetry, fiction, and short story collections. Indie Earth provides its
authors a plethora of services meant to aid them in their book publishing
experiences and finally feel they are releasing the book of their dreams.

With Indie Earth Publishing, you are more than just an author, you are
part of the Indie Earth creative family, making a difference one book at a
time.

www.indieearthbooks.com

For inquiries, please email:
indieearthpublishinghouse@gmail.com

Instagram: @indieearthbooks

Milton Keynes UK
Ingram Content Group UK Ltd.
UKHW010639100823
426647UK00004B/101